To Dwell in Our Midst

A STUDY OF THE TABERNACLE AND HOW IT POINTS US TO JESUS

By
Erin H. Warren

feasting on truth

Copyright © 2022, 2023 by Erin H. Warren
Published by Headley Warren Productions LLC
Orlando, Florida
www.FeastingOnTruth.com

ISBN 978-1-959305-08-8

contents

start here

God desires to be with His people—to be with us. That is the story of the Bible, but that was not the story I believed growing up. I thought the Bible was a collection of stories about some great people and that's what God wanted of me too: to be faithful like Joseph, to be bold like David, to be brave like Esther, to be steadfast like Daniel . . . Oh, yeah, and then Jesus came, and He saved me from my sins. To me, the New Testament was a guide for how to live, and the Old Testament was more of a character study—the things I should do and the things I shouldn't do (such as be bold like David before Goliath, not bold like David on a rooftop). It was a me-centered approach to Scripture.

But then I heard a new term: *the redemptive narrative of Scripture*. It's a churchy way of saying God longs to be with us, and the Bible tells us the story of a God so loving, so faithful, so steadfast, so patient that He would provide the way for this to happen. Our God is a relational God, and He is not content to sit on the outskirts of our lives. He wants to dwell in our midst, and *that* is the story of the Bible.

In Exodus, we find the story of the Israelites, God's chosen people. They were slaves in Egypt under Pharaoh. For over 400 years, they were oppressed and treated ruthlessly. Then God calls a man named Moses to lead them out. Pharaoh refuses nine times, and God sends a plague after each refusal. Then, after one final plague—the death of all the firstborn—Pharaoh relents. The people of Israel leave Egypt bound for the Promised Land—the place God promised their forefather Abraham that his descendants would one day dwell. But first, God leads them into the wilderness where they wander for forty years.

The wilderness is a picture of our relationship with God: saved from slavery and bound for the Promised Land of heaven; but in-between, we are here on earth in a broken world, still marred by sin. This journey is not pointless though. My friend Stacey Thacker says, "The wilderness is the place where the redeemed learn to walk." The wilderness is the place God takes us to show

5

us Himself, to prove His character, and to refine us. It was in this place, the wilderness, that God gave Moses instructions to build a special, holy tent. It is our theme verse for this study:

And let them make me a sanctuary, that I may dwell in their midst.
Exodus 25:8

God was leading the people through the wilderness, but His presence went *before* them in a pillar of cloud by day and a pillar of fire by night. And we see in Exodus 33:7 that anytime Moses wanted to meet with God, he had to do so not only *outside* the camp, but *far away* from the camp. God was with them, but there's a difference between His omnipresence and His nearness in relationship.

The Hebrew word for *dwell* in our theme verse means "to settle down, abide, dwell"[1] and carries the intonation of living with or habitation. There's an implied permanence—this is not a place you come and go, but a place you stay. In fact, the Hebrew word for *tabernacle* means "dwelling place."[2] God was on the outskirts, but He desired to be among His people and in relationship with His people.

BROKEN AND SEPARATED

Understanding this story begins in the first pages of the Bible. In Genesis 1–2, we see the world as it was intended: a place where God dwelled with His creation in a perfect place called Eden. Adam and Eve walked and talked with God every day. They had relationship with God; God was in their midst. There was harmony, joy, peace, kindness. It was good, and there was no sin. Then in Genesis 3:1, Satan enters the garden. He said the same thing to Eve that he still whispers today, "Did God actually say . . . ?"

Sin entered the world, and the relationship between God and man was broken:

Then the LORD God said, "Behold, the man has become like one of us in knowing good and evil. Now, lest he reach out his hand and take also of the tree of life and eat, and live forever—" therefore the LORD God sent him out from the garden of Eden to work the ground from which he was taken. He drove out the man, and at the east of the garden of Eden he placed the cherubim and a flaming sword that turned every way to guard the way to the tree of life.
Genesis 3:22–24

For many years, I missed the love and mercy in those verses. God did not angrily drive out Adam and Eve exclaiming, "If you can't be perfect, then you can't live here!" There were two trees mentioned in Genesis: the tree of knowledge of good and evil and the tree of life. Adam and Eve ate of the tree of knowledge of good and evil, and therefore gained knowledge that was never intended for them or us. God knows good and evil, but He is God. He is righteous, sinless, holy, good, perfect. We are not those things, so knowing good and evil leads to separation. God knew if Adam and Eve ate of the second tree, the tree of life, they would live eternally separated from

1   https://biblehub.com/hebrew/7931.htm
2   https://biblehub.com/hebrew/4908.htm

Him. So, God, in His loving-kindness, drove them out of the garden, because He had a plan. The rest of Scripture reveals that plan.

Why do I tell you all this as an introduction to a study of the Tabernacle? What does the Tabernacle have to do with Jesus dying on the cross? Everything. While all of Scripture reveals the character of God and His desire to be with His people, there are two main stories about how He makes this happen: the story of the Tabernacle and the story of Jesus. They are intertwined, and the former points us to the latter. In fact, as you will discover in this study, the Tabernacle is what the author of Hebrews calls a "shadow": not the true thing, but meant to point us to the True Tent.

The Tabernacle was not perfect or complete. It was temporary. We still needed a Savior. So, God came near and did what we could not accomplish for ourselves:

And the Word became flesh and dwelt among us, and we have seen his glory,
glory as of the only Son from the Father, full of grace and truth.
John 1:14

Do you see the similar language? God came here and "dwelt among us." As we walk through the steps of the Tabernacle and study each furnishing and process, we are going to see a line drawn to Jesus and to our relationship with God. I never fully understood what I was saved from and saved for until studying the Tabernacle. But before I get ahead of myself, let's talk about the study itself.

WHY STUDY INDUCTIVELY?

This study is designed to help provide a foundation for inductive Bible study. When I first heard of inductive study, I was pretty intimidated. But, it's just a fancy term for studying with your own heart and mind first. I honestly didn't even know I *could* study this way until a few years ago at a conference. I had the privilege of hearing one of my favorite Bible teachers speak, and the following quote from her talk forever changed the way I look at Bible study:

We cannot be content being curators of other people's opinions about a book we
can't be bothered to read ourselves. —Jen Wilkin

I realized my entire Christian life I had been a librarian, curating other people's thoughts and beliefs and study findings. It became my driving passion to not only read and study Scripture for myself, but to help other women do the same. I'm so glad you're here! My prayer is that this book helps you:

- Release the bonds of a "perfect quiet time" to find deeper, richer time in the Word

- Build confidence as you learn how to study the Bible firsthand

- Discover truths about God and His character

- See Jesus in the Old Testament

- Grow in your faith and knowledge in a way that produces life change

7

HOW TO USE THIS STUDY

Technically, this is a topical Bible study. I usually prefer studying through chunks of Scripture (whole books or large sections) because you can better understand the context of what you are studying. The Tabernacle instructions and construction are found in several places in the Pentateuch (the first five books of the Bible, also called The Books of Law or The Torah). But additional insight into the meaning and symbolism of this Holy Tent are found throughout all of Scripture. This study is going to take you all over the Bible!

Each week will focus on a different aspect of or furnishing in the Tabernacle with a specific set of questions designed to help you understand and interpret the passages. I use four simple questions as the foundation for any study:

1. What does this say?

2. What does this say about God?

3. What does this mean?

4. How should I respond?

You'll notice that each week isn't broken up into days of study, but rather into these four sections. This allows you the freedom to break up your study week in a way that works with your schedule. I want this time with God to be Holy Spirit-guided, not Erin-guided.

Before your first meeting, take some time to answer the context questions on page 22. Context is crucial when studying Scripture. While this ancient book has not changed and is relevant for us today, we must remember it was written during a different time period and to different people groups. Understanding the cultural context is key to interpreting Scripture. Answering these questions and keeping them at the forefront of your mind as you study will help you better understand what you are reading.

One of the most life-changing aspects of Bible study for me has been asking that second question: "What does this say about God?" as I am studying. This is not a book about us, and particularly in the wilderness, we learn so much about who God is when we ask that question. With each passage you study, you have space to record the names and characteristics of God from that passage. (See pages 17–19 for more information on this.) At the end of each study week, there is a page to record a prayer to God as well as a fill-in-the-blank sentence to help you take His character and apply it to your own life. When we view our life and our circumstances through the lens of His character, we will see lasting change.

The teaching for this Bible study is available on Season 7 of the Feasting on Truth podcast and on YouTube (www.youtube.com/c/erinhwarren). For more information on this study, go to FeastingOnTruth.com/Dwell.

Here are some more tips to help you as you study:

Move Slowly

Many Bible studies plow through Scripture, covering a chapter (or sometimes more) a day. There's certainly a time and a place for that, but I've found when I move through Scripture slowly, reading small sections or focusing on one aspect of the study over the course of one week, the Word of God soaks into my heart and mind deeply. I remember it more easily. I memorize it more effectively. What I love about this particular way of studying is that if I feel the need to stop and let a particular verse sink in, I can do so without feeling like I'm falling behind. It also leaves room for the Holy Spirit to do what only He can do. Which leads me to . . .

Let the Holy Spirit Guide You

Jesus gives us this promise in John 14:26: "But the Helper, the Holy Spirit, whom the Father will send in my name, he will teach you all things and bring to your remembrance all that I have said to you." Anytime I sit down to study, I start with prayer. I ask the Holy Spirit to teach me all the things and to help me remember all the things. That's His job. He's there to help, so invite Him into your time.

Take the Pressure Off

Our time with the Lord doesn't have to be this picture-perfect composition of Bible, notebook, and a cup of coffee (oh how I do love me some good coffee though). The words "quiet time" are not in the Bible, and I've found one size does not fit all. Our time in the Word will change with our stage of life. I tend to deep-dive study about twice a week, but I meditate on it every day. You may sit down and do all of your study in one day or you may devote an hour a day. Find what works for you and stick with it!

Don't Do This Alone

Some of my deepest relationships are ones built on the Word. They are women who gathered around a table or in a living room or online, and we had hard conversations with the Word of Truth between us. Invite a few girlfriends to do this with you. I even included a fun recipe in the back of the book you can make when you get together!

I recommend completing all of the homework on your own before listening to the teaching for the week. You can either listen on your own time or watch together with your group.

Finding time is hard. Women often tell me that they need to put their families first, that work is too crazy, or that they just don't have time to get together with other women for Bible study. Can I challenge you a bit? Is there any time more well spent than investing in our relationship with God? It's hard to pour out from an empty cup. We need to be constantly filled with Jesus, so we can pour out Jesus to our friends, family, and to God. Yes, this may look different in different seasons of life, but you won't regret making it a priority to spend time in the Word with other women.

A LITTLE BACKGROUND INFORMATION

As I mentioned before, context is key before diving into a new Bible study. It helps protect us from misinterpreting what we study. The instructions for the Tabernacle are laid out in several books written by Moses while the Israelites are in the wilderness. The purpose of these books is to tell the people of Israel who they are and who their God is. We will keep this at the forefronts of our minds as we study the Tabernacle. We must also remember that this was not written in the twenty-first century, so there are going to be some difficult passages, particularly around animal sacrifice, that we are going to wrestle through. I want to encourage you to read this with a curious spirit. Do not be afraid to ask questions as you are reading, and be teachable as God reveals Himself in His Word.

The specific plans for the Tabernacle are given to Moses on Mt. Sinai right after God gives the Israelites the Ten Commandments. Many scholars liken this event to a Jewish wedding ceremony. It is God making a covenant, a binding promise, with His people and part of that is defining what their relationship is going to look like. In Jewish weddings, it is called a ketubah, and here's what I find most fascinating: it was usually for the bride's protection. So, when we look at these laws, regulations, and commands, we should remember that they are what define us as God's people and they are for our benefit. We are meant to be set apart, to look different than the world around us, and it is our relationship with God and His dwelling in our midst that does it.

COMPANION TEACHINGS AND OTHER RESOURCES

I am committed to walking alongside you as you study Scripture inductively. I know you can do this, and I want to help you be successful. With the purchase of this book, I'm offering you access to what I'm calling *The Alongside Guide*. Scan the QR code or visit FeastingOnTruth.com/Dwell. There, you can sign up to access this valuable study bonus. You'll receive an email for each week of study  with helpful resources, including links to that week's teaching video and podcast, study notes with cross-references, quotes, characteristics of God, small group discussion questions, and more. It's everything you need to be successful in your study, and it gets delivered right to your inbox.

LET'S FEAST!

In the wilderness, God showed the people how to be in relationship with Him, and He does the same for us today. It is the place we learn what it looks like to walk with God. That is why Jesus came—not to give us a "get out of hell free card"—but to be the Way Maker. He opened the way for us to have relationship with God, for God to dwell in our midst.

Can I give you one big spoiler? As we trace the steps through the Tabernacle, they will form the shape of a cross. Jesus is at the heart of all of Scripture, and I am so excited to have you alongside on this journey. It is my prayer that through this study, you will see just how madly in love with you God is.

Because of Christ,

Erin H. Warren

10

four simple questions

Good Bible study is rooted in asking the right questions of Scripture. Our first inclination in Bible study is often to ask, "What does this mean to me?" We want to cut right to the ending. Instead, learning to first understand the context, summary, and character of God in the passage will better help us discern the meaning and our response. I have adopted what I call *Four Simple Questions* as the foundation of my time in the Word. Yes, this takes a little more time and effort, but the practice of persevering through the Word is a valuable one. These four simple questions, as well as other helpful tips and resources for inductive study, are further explained in my book, *Feasting on Truth: Savor the Life-giving Word of God.*

START WITH CONTEXT

It's important to remember that while the Bible was written for us and is applicable to our lives today (Hebrews 4:12), we are not the original audience. It is a book not written in modern America, but in the ancient Middle East. If we do not first answer some key questions to understand the context, we cannot properly understand the passage and its intent. Most of these answers can be found in a good study Bible.

FOUR SIMPLE QUESTIONS

I realized that one of my downfalls when attempting to read and study the Bible for myself was not knowing which questions to ask. Many of the methods I tried were either too open or too rigid. Asking four simple questions provided the right balance of structure and flexibility I needed. I want to release you from thinking this has to look a certain way—it doesn't. Basically: Are you showing up? Are you changing? Are you connected? Does that make you want to keep showing up? If you answer yes to all of these, then you're on the right track! Here is a brief overview of each question:

11

1. **What does this say?**
   Before we can interpret Scripture, we need to know what's going on in the passage. Some methods would call this *observation* or the *aim of the passage*.

   - Write a 1–2 sentence summary of what the passage is about—no interpretation, just the facts.

   - Answer the questions: Who? What? Where? When?

   - Are there any repeated words or phrases?

   - Are there any transitional words (therefore, so, but, and, etc.)? Remember, every word is there for a reason.

2. **What does this say about God?**
   This to me has been the most transformative question to ask during Bible study. This book is not about us; it's about God. His character and name are written on every page. Before we can understand our response, we must know who He is.

   - What names of God are used? (His names speak to His character.)

   - What characteristics of God are in this passage?

   - I include Jesus in this as well: What does this passage tell us about Jesus?

   - You can find lists of the names and characteristics of God on pages 18–19.

   - Each week, complete the sentence "Because God is _____, I can _____."

3. **What does this mean?**
   PRAY. PRAY. PRAY. Ask the Holy Spirit to guide you in this. Using context, the summary, and other observations you have made, begin to be a detective. Remember the lens through which you are looking. Yes, this takes work, but it's worth doing!

   - Read the passage in multiple translations. What differences do you see?

   - Look up words in the English dictionary.

   - What other passages in Scripture are related to this one? (These are called cross-references.)

   - Read a trusted commentary or study Bible.

   - Research the original language (the Old Testament was originally written in Hebrew and the New Testament in Greek).

   - Go to FeastingOnTruth.com/Resources for recommended resources, Bibles, and commentaries.

4. **How should I respond?**
   Our Bible study should change us. John 17:17 says, "Sanctify them in the truth; your word is truth." *Sanctify* is a big churchy word that means "to purify or to make holy." It's the act of separating ourselves from the actions of our flesh and dedicating more of our lives and actions to God. God's Word has a purpose in our lives (Isaiah 55:10–11), and we shouldn't stop at knowing its meaning. Instead, we should respond:

   - Is there an action I need to take?

- A conversation I need to have?

- A moment of worship?

- Something I should let go?

- Write out a prayer.

However you feel led to respond, write it down and enlist someone to hold you accountable.

OTHER HELPFUL TIPS

Listen to the Passage

Use a Bible app to listen to the passages each week. We often feel like this is a cop-out, but for thousands of years, the Word of God was passed down orally from generation to generation. It's a book meant to be read out loud, and when you listen to it, you'll be amazed at how much you pick up on that you didn't notice when reading it.

Use Different Colored Pens

I've found using different colored pens when writing my study notes helps me remember where the note came from. For instance, I use different colors for rewriting the Scripture verses, my thoughts, certain study Bibles, cross-references or different translations, commentary quotes, and Greek or Hebrew word definitions. I don't really have a color system, so the colors change from time to time. That's okay too!

Start with a Clean Copy of God's Word

A study Bible adds additional commentary. Using a Bible that doesn't have any additional commentary removes the temptation to peek at notes before fully understanding the passage on your own. If you do not have a non-study Bible, don't fret! You can print out chapters on several Bible websites including www.BibleGateway.com. I use an ESV journaling Bible for my initial study (which has very few footnotes), then move to other versions and other study Bibles as I go through my study week. Speaking of translations . . .

A Note About Translations

There are a myriad of translations out there, so how do you know which to pick? First, it's important to know where translations come from. The Old Testament was originally written in Hebrew, while the New Testament was written in Greek (though a few portions were written in Aramaic).

Over the years, translators have used original copies written in these languages to interpret Scripture into English (and other languages as well). Translations fall on a spectrum between two ends: word-for-word (translations that use the closest English word to the original word) and thought-for-thought (translations that rephrase the words into more modern, understandable English). Technically, all of them are a mix of the two, but some lean more toward one end or the other.

Some examples of translations that lean toward word-for-word include: English Standard Version (ESV—my top choice), New American Standard Bible (NAS or NASB), and King James Version (KJV). These are the closest to the original language, but we can sometimes miss the cultural context.

An example of thought-for-thought is the New Living Translation (NLT).

There are also versions that are more toward the middle of the spectrum, such as the Christian Standard Bible (CSB) and the New International Version (NIV).

The last kind of translation is not necessarily a translation at all, but rather a paraphrase. Paraphrase Bibles, like *The Message*, should be treated more like commentary because, while they can bring insight into the meaning of the passage, they are not Scripture themselves. I rarely use this type. If you do use a paraphrase, wait until you've completed questions 1–3 and are consulting other commentaries for additional insights.

Welcome to the Feast!

See? Simple. Yes, it takes practice, but honestly, it doesn't take as long as you'd think. You just have to be willing to spend time with Jesus. In Acts 4, Peter and John are on trial before the religious leaders (the smartest of the smart when it came to the Law), and in verse 13 it says, "Now when they saw the boldness of Peter and John, and perceived that they were uneducated, common men, they were astonished. And they recognized that they had been with Jesus." Uneducated. Common. Peter and John hadn't been to seminary, but they had been *with* Jesus.

What I've found is that there is not one method that will make all of this work for you. The power is not in the method. The power is in the Word of God. The power is in spending time with Jesus in the Word with the Holy Spirit as your guide.

When you see your life change and you find community around the Word, you will find yourself returning to Scripture, growing more confident as you study, and discovering the joy and excitement of Feasting on Truth.

Visit FeastingOnTruth.com/HowTo for more information
and in-depth teachings on these questions.

small group guide

I am a firm believer in gathering together around the Word of God. It is at the heart of Feasting on Truth. As stated in *start here*, I believe that small group discussion is incredibly important when studying the Bible. I heard a pastor say, "Our time in the Word should be personal but never private." I do not believe we are called to study in isolation, and I believe it is in those places of isolation where Satan loves to tempt us. Discussing the passage in a small group setting (even if it's with only one other woman) helps confirm what the Holy Spirit taught you. It holds us accountable to truth. Not only that, but I learn so much from other women too. They will see truths within those passages that I miss. It helps build layers of understanding.

Leading a group is not nearly as difficult as it seems. I like to think of group leaders more like discussion leaders. A great discussion leader talks less than a third of the group time. You may need to speak first or jump in to get the conversation going, but the goal is to get the group talking.

Teaching for each chapter is available on Season 7 of the Feasting on Truth podcast or my YouTube channel: YouTube.com/c/erinhwarren.

Here are some other tips and a guide for your small group time:

Lead with authenticity
You do not have to have all the answers or have it all together to lead. I do not have it all together, and I fail miserably every day at doing what I know I should (Romans 7!). But I don't have to air all my dirty laundry to be authentic, and I never want my authenticity to enable sin in other people's lives. I've found that when I'm real about where I am and I invite women in to see how God is working on me in those areas, it invites them into authentic life change as well.

Set up a group text or use a group chat app
Connection throughout the week is key to building connection within your group. If you are not tech savvy or keeping up with a group chat isn't your strength, ask someone in the group to take charge of that. It's a great way to get others involved too! Throughout the week, you can check in on your group or share a verse or a particular insight into the passage.

Start with an ice breaker question
It doesn't have to be deep or spiritual, just something to get the conversation flowing. These types of questions are always a great way to help a group of women get to know each other.

15

Share your summary

Have the women share their summary for that week's passage. Depending on the size of your group, you may want to limit this to two to three women.

Ask: What characteristics of God did you see in this week's passage?

This works well "popcorn style." Let the women jump in with various names and characteristics of God and the verses that correspond. I usually add these to my own notes as well.

Use the weekly discussion questions

There are discussion questions marked within each week's homework. For additional weekly discussion questions, go to FeastingOnTruth.com/Dwell and sign up to receive *The Alongside Guide* in your email. Each week, you'll get additional questions (as well as other resources and notes) delivered right to your inbox.

Share "Because God is" statements

This is a simple one, and I love it when everyone shares theirs! Depending on how long you have been together, some women in your group may not feel comfortable sharing the nitty-gritty of their lives. Having everyone share their "Because God is" statement is a way to engage the women who do not feel comfortable speaking up.

Share prayer requests

Sharing what is going on in our lives opens the door to build community and meet needs. I'll never forget sitting in a group when a woman shared that she needed prayer that she could pass her driving test. Across the table, another woman in the group spoke up and said, "I can help you learn to drive!" A couple months later, I received a picture of the two women holding a brand-new driver's license. It was incredible! Praying for one another is commanded, so allow time for this with your group. Pray with one another. Pray throughout the week. When we do this, we get to share an inheritance in what God is doing through the lives of others.

GROUP LIST

NAME	PHONE	EMAIL

knowing God

For too many years, I struggled with knowing how to interpret Scripture and apply these ancient words to my life. I did not know that God promises to equip us in studying Scripture through the Holy Spirit. And truthfully, I treated my Bible like one of those balls you shake, ask a question, flip over, and find your answer. Too many times I came to Scripture looking for an answer to my question, or I treated it like a yearbook—looking for all the pictures of myself.

Then, I began asking a different question, and my entire Bible study and life changed. I asked, "What does this say about God?" This shifted my perspective from a self-centered approach toward Scripture (where I am always asking, "What does this mean *to* me or *for* me?") to a God-centered approach—intentionally looking for and seeking out what each passage teaches me about God.

The Bible is not about me. It is first and foremost a book about God, and His name and character are written across every page. Our purpose on earth is to know God and make Him known, to love God and love others. But we can't love what we don't know; we can't worship what we don't know. And the primary way we know God is through His Word. The pursuit of knowledge about God is not optional; it's essential.

On the following pages, you will find two lists to help you: Names of God and Characteristics of God. It's not comprehensive, and there are spaces for you to add others as you discover more with each passage you read. Here are ways you can have a God-centered approach to your study:

- Ask, "What characteristics of God do I see in this passage?"

- Ask, "What names of God do I see in this passage?" (His names speak to His character.)

- Complete this sentence: Because God is _____, I can _____.

I understand there are different roles of the Trinity (God the Father, God the Son, God the Holy Spirit), but for the sake of simplicity (and especially as you are beginning), I think of them as One. If you need further help, visit www.FeastingOnTruth.com for more information and resources.

names of God

Abba Father

Adonai *(Lord, Master)*

Alpha and Omega

Bread of Life

Chief Cornerstone

Creator

Deliverer

El Elyon *(The Most High God)*

El Olam *(The Everlasting God)*

El Roi *(The God Who Sees Me)*

El Shaddai *(The Lord God Almighty)*

Elohim

Emmanuel

Everlasting Father

Great High Priest

Holy One

I AM

King of Kings

Lamb of God

Light of the World

Lion of Judah

Lord of Lords

Mighty God

Morning Star

Prince of Peace

Resurrection and the Life

Savior

Wonderful Counselor

Yahweh Amen *(The Lord is Truth)*

Yahweh Jireh *(The Lord Provides)*

Yahweh Nissi *(The Lord is my Banner)*

Yahweh-Raah *(The Lord is my Shepherd)*

Yahweh Rapha *(The Lord Heals)*

Yahweh Shalom *(The Lord is Peace)*

characteristics of God

Abounding in Steadfast Love

Compassionate

Deliberate

Faithful

Forgiving

Full of Grace

Good

Glorious

Gracious

Guide

Holy

Immutable *(Unchanging)*

Infinite

Invisible

Jealous

Just

Kind

Long-Suffering/Patient

Love

Merciful

Mighty

Omnipotent *(All-Powerful)*

Omnipresent

Omniscient *(All-Knowing)*

One

Perfect

Protector

Provider

Refuge/Help

Righteous

Self-Sufficient

Slow to Anger

Sovereign

Trustworthy

Truth

Wise

With Us

THE TABERNACLE

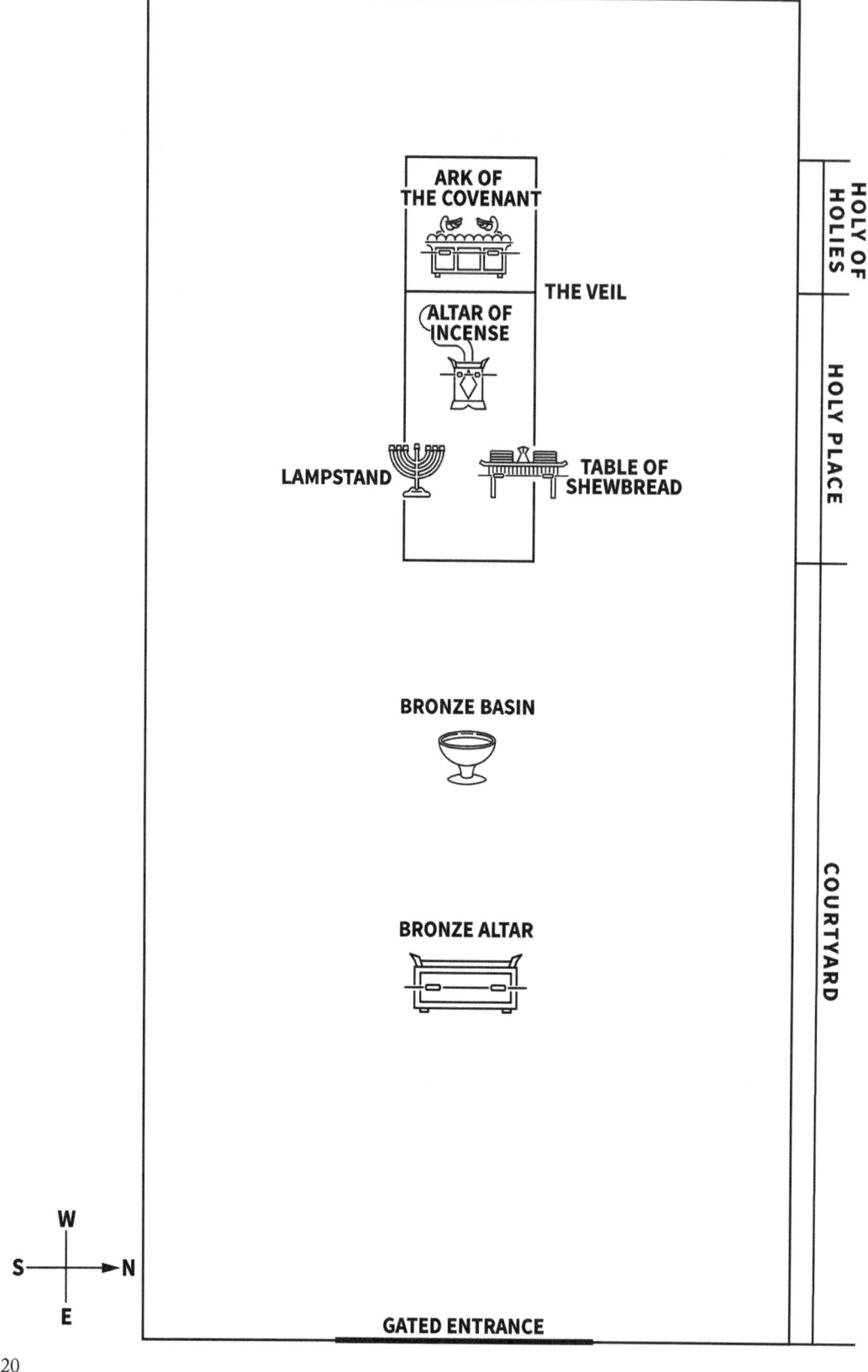

ARK OF THE COVENANT

THE VEIL

ALTAR OF INCENSE

LAMPSTAND

TABLE OF SHEWBREAD

HOLY OF HOLIES

HOLY PLACE

BRONZE BASIN

BRONZE ALTAR

COURTYARD

W — S — N — E

GATED ENTRANCE

To Dwell in Our Midst

CONTEXT

Who wrote the first five books of the Bible?

What do you know about this author?

To whom were these books written?

When were they written?

What is the genre of these books?

What was the intent or purpose?

What was going on in history when they were written?

What do you know about the Tabernacle?

To Dwell in our Midst

CONTEXT NOTES

TO Dwell IN OUR Midst

TEACHING NOTES

To Dwell in our Midst

TEACHING NOTES

To Dwell in our Midst

GROUP NOTES

To Dwell in our Midst

WEEK 1

THE PURPOSE AND CONTRIBUTIONS

WHAT DOES THIS SAY?

The Presence of God

READ EXODUS 13:17-22

Who was leading the Israelites?

Where did He lead them?

How was He leading them?

READ EXODUS 33:7-17

Where did Moses go to meet with God?

What is Moses asking of God in these verses?

Why was it so important that God's presence go with His people?

How does God respond?

DISCUSSION: How does God's dwelling in our midst set us apart today?

Write out Deuteronomy 2:7.

What does God's presence provide for us?

Purpose of the Tabernacle

READ EXODUS 25:1-9

Write out Exodus 25:8.

What materials were the people to contribute?

DISCUSSION: What is the purpose of the Tabernacle? (v. 8, see also Exodus 29:42–46) How does this change or enhance your understanding of God?

According to v. 9, how are they to construct the Tabernacle? What does this tell you about God's character in light of the purpose of the Tabernacle?

Contributions to the Tabernacle

READ EXODUS 35:4–29

Write a 1–2 sentence summary of these verses.

What new insights do you gain about the contributions for the Tabernacle?

Read Exodus 11:2–3 and 12:33–36. Where did the Israelites get these materials and skills?

DISCUSSION: How do you think their roles as slaves prepared them for the building of the Tabernacle? What does this tell us about God's ability to provide and use our circumstances for His glory?

The phrase "whose heart stirred" is used multiple times in this passage. What do you think that means?

Read Colossians 3:23–24. How were the Israelites reflecting this verse?

The Artists

READ EXODUS 35:30–36:7

Summarize these verses in 1–2 sentences.

Who did God call to build the Tabernacle?
How did he receive this gift? (vv. 31–35)

How did the people respond to the request for contributions? What did Moses command in Exodus 36:6 as a result?

WHAT DOES THIS SAY ABOUT GOD?

What characteristics of God do you see in this week's study?

WHAT DOES THIS MEAN?

Jesus, The True Tent

READ HEBREWS 8:1–7

Who is the author of Hebrews talking about here?

Who built the Tabernacle vs. who built the true tent? Why is that significant?

According to the author of Hebrews, what is the original Tabernacle?

Reread Exodus 25:8–9. How does Hebrews 8:5 add to your understanding of the Exodus verses?

DISCUSSION: Why (as stated in v. 7) is the first covenant with fault?

TO Dwell IN OUR Midst

WEEK 1 NOTES

To Dwell in our Midst

WEEK 1 NOTES

To Dwell in our Midst

WEEK 1 NOTES

HOW SHOULD I RESPOND?

What was the purpose of the Tabernacle? How did God provide for His people in order for them to follow His instructions? How have you seen Him do that for you today?

Write a prayer of praise and thanksgiving for how Jesus is the more and better tent.

Because God is:

    I can:

To Dwell in our Midst

TEACHING NOTES

To Dwell in our Midst

TEACHING NOTES

To Dwell in our Midst

GROUP NOTES

The Priestly Garments

READ EXODUS 28

Write a 2–3 sentence summary of this passage.

What are the pieces of the priestly garments?

What symbolism do you see in the garments?

What is the role of the priests? (Numbers 3:6–7) What is the role of the high priest? (Exodus 28:29–30; 35)

To Dwell in our Midst

WEEK 2

THE BRONZE ALTAR

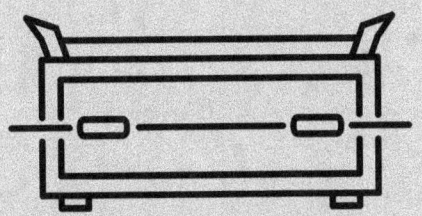

WHAT DOES THIS SAY?

Look up the following words in the dictionary and write out their definitions:

Holy:

Sanctify:

Consecrate:

Atonement:

READ EXODUS 27:1–8 AND 38:1–7

Summarize these verses in 1–2 sentences.

What are the dimensions and shape of the Bronze Altar?

What was it made of?

What other details and utensils are part of the construction of the altar?

What do you notice about the way Moses writes the plans in the first section and the way he writes the process by which it was built? Why do you think he wrote it this way?

WHAT DOES THIS SAY ABOUT GOD?

What characteristics of God do you see in this week's study?

WHAT DOES THIS MEAN?

The Sacrifices

(see page 142 for the answer key)

OLD TESTAMENT SCRIPTURE	TYPE OF OFFERING	PURPOSE	WHAT WAS OFFERED	NEW TESTAMENT SCRIPTURE	REFLECTING JESUS
Leviticus 1:1–4, 10, 14 Leviticus 6:8–13				Romans 12:1–2	
Leviticus 2:1–3, 8–13 Leviticus 6:14–18				Hebrews 4:15 (see 1 Corinthians 5:6–8 for what leaven represents)	
Leviticus 3:1–2, 6–8, 12–13 Leviticus 7:11–13, 28–30				John 6:53–58 John 15:8–11	
Leviticus 4:1–3, 13–15, 22–24, 27–29 5:1–7, 11 6:24–25				Romans 5:1–11 Romans 3:23	
Leviticus 5:14–16, 17–19 6:1–7 7:1–2				Isaiah 53:4–6 Colossians 1:13–14 Ephesians 1:7–10	

Read Leviticus 17:11. Why is the shedding of blood necessary to make atonement?

DISCUSSION: Why is atonement necessary for us to approach God?

READ LEVITICUS 9

In what order does Aaron sacrifice the offerings?

9:8 –

9:12 –

9:15 –

9:16 –

9:17 –

9:18 –

Using the chart, what is significant about the order?

Why is it significant that Aaron first present the sin and burnt offerings to atone for himself and his sons before offering the sin offering for the people?

How did the people respond in v. 24 to God accepting their offering?

DISCUSSION: What parallels do you see between the sacrifices and our daily Christian walk?

Jesus, Our Priest & Sacrifice

READ HEBREWS 7:11–28

What similar language do you see describing Jesus and the sacrifices named in Exodus and Leviticus?

In the Old Testament, who offered the sacrifices? What did they offer as sacrifices? In the New Testament, who offered the sacrifice? What did He offer?

Read Hebrews 10:1–10. According to this passage, why are the Old Testament sacrifices insufficient? How is Jesus a more and better sacrifice?

To Dwell in our Midst

WEEK 2 NOTES

49

To Dwell in our Midst

WEEK 2 NOTES

50

HOW SHOULD I RESPOND?

What is the first furnishing encountered in the Tabernacle? What was the purpose? What did this accomplish?

Write a prayer of praise and thanksgiving for how Jesus is the more and better sacrifice.

Because God is:

I can:

To Dwell in our Midst

TEACHING NOTES

To Dwell in our Midst

TEACHING NOTES

To Dwell in our Midst

GROUP NOTES

TO Dwell IN OUR Midst

WEEK 3

THE BRONZE BASIN

WHAT DOES THIS SAY?

READ EXODUS 30:17–21 AND 38:8

Summarize these verses in 1–2 sentences.

What is the Bronze Basin made of?

What is the purpose of the basin?

What difference do you see between the instructions for the Bronze Basin and the other pieces of the Tabernacle we've studied?

Why do you think the Basin came after the Bronze Altar?

DISCUSSION: Why was it important that the priests cleansed themselves before entering the Holy Place?

Why do you think Moses included the additional detail in Exodus 38:8?

WHAT DOES THIS SAY ABOUT GOD?

What characteristics of God do you see in this week's study?

WHAT DOES THIS MEAN?

The Stain of Sin

Cultural Side Note: glass had not been invented yet, but Egyptians used highly polished bronze or brass to create mirrors. Some of these are on display in the British Museum in London today!

What is the purpose of a mirror?

DISCUSSION: Why would it be useful to have a basin made of mirrors?

Read Psalm 26:6, Psalm 73:13, and Matthew 27:24. Symbolically, what did the washing of hands mean?

Read 1 John 1:5–10. DISCUSSION: How does walking in light have the same effect as looking in a mirror at our own sin? What does this look like practically? How does fellowship with one another play a role in our "cleansing"?

Blood & Water

READ LEVITICUS 14:48–53

In your Bible, what is the heading for this chapter?

CONTEXT: Leviticus is a collection of laws for the Israelites to remain pure and clean. Reading this particular passage, what two liquids are required to make the house clean after leprosy? *(The hyssop and cedarwood are symbolic as well, but we are focusing on these two liquids in this study.)*

What does each symbolically do?

How do we see the same idea in the Tabernacle thus far? What is the purpose of the sacrifice and the purpose of the cleansing?

DISCUSSION: Why is cleansing and making clean so important to God?

Jesus Cleanses and Sanctifies

READ JOHN 19:31–37

What flowed out of Jesus when His side was pierced on the cross? How does this fulfill what we see in the Tabernacle?

DISCUSSION: Why do you think both blood and water are necessary? What role does each one play?

Read Ephesians 5:25–27. What does this passage say Christ did for us? What is the washing of water compared to? (You may want to reference the definition of *sanctify* from Week 2.)

Read John 17:17–19. How does Jesus say we are sanctified?

DISCUSSION: Why is it important to know the Word?

Read Isaiah 55:6–11. What does the Word do for us? What does this passage tell us about ourselves in comparison to God?

DISCUSSION: What is the difference between studying the Bible and knowing the Bible?

DISCUSSION: How can we read and study His Word in a way that changes and sanctifies us?

READ EZEKIEL 36:22–29

What does this tell you about God's holy name?

What is God's plan for us according to this passage?

To Dwell in our Midst

TO Dwell IN OUR Midst

WEEK 3 NOTES

HOW SHOULD I RESPOND?

What is the second furnishing encountered in the Tabernacle? What was the purpose? What did this accomplish?

Write a prayer of praise and thanksgiving for how Jesus is the more and better sanctification.

Because God is:

    I can:

To Dwell in our Midst

TEACHING NOTES

To Dwell in our Midst

TEACHING NOTES

To Dwell in our Midst

GROUP NOTES

Go to BibleGateway.com, type "water" into the search bar at the top of the page, and select "English Standard Version". On the right-hand side of the screen, you will see "filter by" and all the books of the Bible. Click "Leviticus". How many times does the word "water" appear in Leviticus? As you scroll through the verses, what theme do you see about the purpose of water?

To Dwell in Our Midst

WEEK 4

THE LAMPSTAND

WHAT DOES THIS SAY?

READ EXODUS 25:31–40 AND EXODUS 37:17–24

Write a 1–2 sentence summary of these passages.

What was the Lampstand made of?

How was it created?

What five parts were to be on the branches?

How many branches were there?

How many lamps were on the stand?

How much gold was used? (See the footnote in your Bible for how heavy that was!)

WHAT DOES THIS SAY ABOUT GOD?

What characteristics of God do you see in this week's study?

WHAT DOES THIS MEAN?

Think back to the design of the Tabernacle and the Holy Place (Exodus 26:14). Why would a Lampstand be important? Why would it be the first step upon entering?

The Tree

READ NUMBERS 17

Write a 2–3 sentence summary of this passage.

What similarities do you see between the Lampstand and Aaron's budded staff?

What do you think Aaron's staff was made of? Knowing this, what symbolism might the Lampstand have?

READ ISAIAH 11:1–5, 10

Who is Jesse? (Matthew 1:1–6) Who do you think is the "shoot from the stump of Jesse"?

How does this passage describe Him?

According to v. 10, what will this "root of Jesse" be for the people?

Jesus, The True Vine

READ JOHN 15:1–11

What does this say about our ability to bear fruit?

DISCUSSION: Notice in v. 3 what has already happened in order that we may bear fruit? How does this add to your understanding of the order of process in the Tabernacle?

The Oil

READ EXODUS 27:20–21 AND LEVITICUS 24:1–4 *in the English Standard Version (ESV)*

What additional details do you see about the Lampstand in the Leviticus passage?

What two words describe the process by which the oil is made? How does this reflect God's character?

What was the purpose of the oil in the Lampstand?

Read Isaiah 61:1 and Acts 10:36–38. What does oil symbolize?

The Holy Spirit, Our Helper

READ JOHN 16:13-15

What is the purpose of the Holy Spirit?

DISCUSSION: How does this passage explain how the Holy Spirit helps us?

Reread Isaiah 11:1–2. Label the lamp based on these verses. (Hint: look at the pattern of the "spirit of . . .")

DISCUSSION: Where have you been relying on your own understanding in your circumstances instead of trusting the Holy Spirit to be your Helper? Which one aspect of the Spirit named in Isaiah 11:1–2 do you want to focus on this week?

The Light

What is the practical purpose of the Lampstand in the Holy Place? Who was allowed in the Holy Place to see this light?

Jesus, The Light of the World

READ JOHN 1:1-14

Who is this passage talking about?

List all of the characteristics of the Word we see in this passage.

Read John 8:12. What does Jesus call Himself? What is a result of His light?

DISCUSSION: How is the light of the Lampstand similar to the light of Jesus? How is Jesus' light different?

To Dwell in our Midst

WEEK 4 NOTES

To Dwell in our Midst

WEEK 4 NOTES

HOW SHOULD I RESPOND?

What is the third furnishing encountered in the Tabernacle? What was the purpose? What did this accomplish?

Write a prayer of praise and thanksgiving for how Jesus is the more and better lampstand.

Because God is:

    I can:

To Dwell in our Midst

TEACHING NOTES

To Dwell in our Midst

TEACHING NOTES

To Dwell in our Midst

GROUP NOTES

TO Dwell IN OUR Midst
GROUP NOTES

The Light of the Church

READ REVELATION 1:9–20

Write a 2–3 sentence summary of this passage.

Who is writing this? Where is he?

What characteristics of Jesus are listed here?

In this vision, what does the Lampstand represent?

Think back to the construction of the Lampstand in Exodus 25:31–40. What characteristics of the church are reflected in the Lampstand?

READ REVELATION 2:1-7

What warning does Jesus give the church at Ephesus?

What will their punishment be?

Read Matthew 5:14–16. How can we not lose our first love and let our light shine for His glory?

To Dwell in our Midst

WEEK 5

THE TABLE OF SHEWBREAD

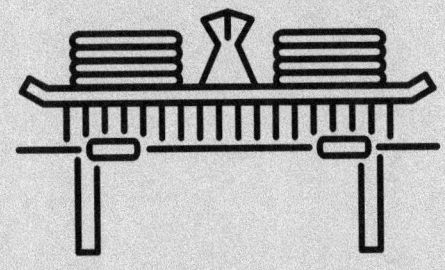

WHAT DOES THIS SAY?

READ EXODUS 25:23-30 AND EXODUS 37:10-16

Write a 1–2 sentence summary of these verses.

What two materials was the table made of?

What are the details of its dimensions and design?

What detail does Scripture give us about its portability?

What other accessories are part of the construction of the table and what are they for?

WHAT DOES THIS SAY ABOUT GOD?

What characteristics of God do you see in this week's study?

WHAT DOES THIS MEAN?

The Bread

READ LEVITICUS 24:5–9

How is the bread made?

How is the bread arranged? What is significant about the number of loaves?

Where does the bread come from? (See Leviticus 2:1–3 for review.)

Why did Aaron and his sons eat the bread? Where did they eat it? (See Numbers 1:47–54, Deuteronomy 10:8–9 for more insight.)

DISCUSSION: Why do think purity and holiness are so important to God?

DISCUSSION: Which day were the priests to replace the bread? Why do think this particular day was God's chosen day for the task?

Think about physical bread, particularly in that time period. What is its purpose?

Jesus, the Bread of Life
READ JOHN 6:22–59

Write a 2–3 sentence summary of this passage.

CONTEXT: What miracle took place the day before this story? (John 6:1–14)

Why did Jesus say the people were coming to Him?

DISCUSSION: How is Jesus the better manna? (How is manna a shadow of Jesus? Think also about the purpose of the Tabernacle.)

DISCUSSION: In what ways do we come to God for our physical needs instead of seeking Him for our spiritual needs?

According to vv. 56–57, what do we gain in having a relationship with Jesus?

READ JOHN 6:60–71

How did some of those following Jesus respond to Jesus' reply?

How did Simon Peter respond?

DISCUSSION: How is Jesus our essential nourishment and sustenance for life? What are the things we often turn to for temporary satisfaction?

The Fellowship of Believers
READ LUKE 22:7–20
Summarize this passage in 2–3 sentences.

Why do we partake of bread together in the Lord's Supper? In light of this week's study, what does this remind us of?

READ ACTS 2:42–47

Summarize this passage in 2–3 sentences.

What did the "breaking of bread" symbolize?

What was the posture of the believers' hearts?

DISCUSSION: Why is it important that we keep Jesus at the center of our fellowship within the family of God?

To Dwell in our Midst

WEEK 5 NOTES

To Dwell in our Midst

WEEK 5 NOTES

HOW SHOULD I RESPOND?

What is the fourth furnishing encountered in the Tabernacle? What was the purpose? What did this accomplish?

Write a prayer of praise and thanksgiving for how Jesus is the more and better bread and the more and better communion.

Because God is:

    I can:

94

To Dwell in our Midst

TEACHING NOTES

TO Dwell IN OUR Midst

TEACHING NOTES

To Dwell in our Midst

GROUP NOTES

To Dwell in our Midst

GROUP NOTES

To Dwell in our Midst

WEEK 6

THE ALTAR OF INCENSE

WHAT DOES THIS SAY?

READ EXODUS 30:1-10 AND 37:25-29

What are the dimensions of the Altar of Incense?

What materials were used in its construction?

What other details does Moses give about its design and placement in the Holy Place?

When was the offering of incense given?

What warning does God give Moses in v. 9?

In addition to the daily tending, what was Aaron to do one time a year on the Day of Atonement?

DISCUSSION: Think back over the whole study. Each piece served a practical purpose but also a spiritual purpose. Why do you think incense would be beneficial practically?

WHAT DOES THIS SAY ABOUT GOD?

What characteristics of God do you see in this week's study?

WHAT DOES THIS MEAN?

The Incense

Write the definitions for these words (see Week 2 for review):

Atonement:

Holy:

Pure:

READ EXODUS 30:34-38

What spices make up the mix for the incense?

How much of each spice was to be used?

BONUS: Look up each spice and write what it was. You can also type them in the search bar on BibleGateway.com to see where else these spices are mentioned in the Bible.

How many times does the word "pure" occur in these verses? How many times is the word "holy" used?

What does this tell us about God's character?

DISCUSSION: Both "pure" and "holy" are used to describe the salt. Salt was also used in bread (see Leviticus 2:13). Knowing what you know about salt, why do you think it was an important component?

Holy & Pure Sacrifice

READ LEVITICUS 10:1-11

Why did Aaron's sons die?

Why did Moses give such specific instructions to Mishael and Elzaphan about how to remove the bodies?

DISCUSSION: What does this tell us about God's holiness?

READ MALACHI 1:1-14

What kind of sacrifices were the people offering God?

What was their request in v. 9?

What do you think it means to "kindle fire on my altar in vain"?

What is God's response?

DISCUSSION: In what ways do we approach God with less than the best? How can we guard against the temptation to do so? How should we approach God?

The Interceding

READ PSALM 141:2, REVELATION 5:8, AND REVELATION 8:3-4

What does the incense represent?

Look up the following words in the dictionary and write their definition:

Prayer:

Interceding:

Intercessor:

DISCUSSION: Given these definitions and the symbolism of the incense, how is the priest acting as an intercessor for the people?

Jesus, Our Intercessor

READ HEBREWS 7:22–28

What does this passage tell us about Jesus?

What does He "always live" to do?

DISCUSSION: How is Jesus' intercession for us better than the priests of the Tabernacle?

READ ROMANS 8:31–39

Where is Christ, and what is he doing according to this passage?

READ ROMANS 8:26-27

What does the Holy Spirit do according to this passage?

DISCUSSION: How does knowing Jesus and the Holy Spirit are interceding for you encourage you in your prayer life?

Interceding for One Another

READ 1 TIMOTHY 2:1-7

Write a 1–2 sentence summary of these verses.

Who is our mediator?

What part do we play?

DISCUSSION: According to this passage, why do we pray?

READ EPHESIANS 6:10-18

Write a 2–3 sentence summary of these verses.

DISCUSSION: Why do you think Paul includes prayer as part of the Armor of God and our defense against the devil?

When are we to pray? Who are we to pray for?

READ 1 PETER 2:1-10

Write a 2–3 sentence summary of these verses.

As a child of God, what are we "being built up as"? For what purpose?

What four descriptors does Peter use to describe the people of God in v. 9?

In vv. 9–10, what benefits do we have as God's chosen people?

DISCUSSION: How are we like the priests (mediators of God's covenant) to the world around us?

To Dwell in our Midst

WEEK 6 NOTES

To Dwell in our Midst

WEEK 6 NOTES

HOW SHOULD I RESPOND?

What is the fifth furnishing encountered in the Tabernacle? What was the purpose? What did this accomplish?

Write a prayer of praise and thanksgiving for how Jesus is the more and better intercessor.

Because God is:

I can:

To Dwell in our Midst

TEACHING NOTES

To Dwell in our Midst

TEACHING NOTES

To Dwell in our Midst

GROUP NOTES

To Dwell in our Midst

WEEK 7

THE ARK OF THE COVENANT

WHAT DOES THIS SAY?

The Veil

READ EXODUS 26:31–34

What was the veil made of?

What was woven into the curtain?

How was it hung?

What was the purpose of the veil?

The Ark of the Covenant

READ EXODUS 25:10–16 AND EXODUS 37:1–5

What were the dimensions of the Ark of the Covenant?

What materials was it made from?

What additional detail does God give about the poles? How is this different than the other furnishings in the Tabernacle? Why do you think this is?

What does God tell Moses to put into the ark? (v. 16; read the NIV or CSB version for more detail.)

The Mercy Seat

READ EXODUS 25:17–22 AND EXODUS 37:6–9

Read v. 17 in NIV. What is another name for the mercy seat?

What material was the mercy seat made from?

What adorned the top of the mercy seat? What unique details are given about them?

What did God say would happen at the mercy seat?

Before this study, what did you think of the Ark, Holy of Holies, or Veil? What new insights do you have now? How do you see God's purity/holiness reiterated in these three elements of the Tabernacle?

WHAT DOES THIS SAY ABOUT GOD?

What characteristics of God do you see in this week's study?

WHAT DOES THIS MEAN?

The Day of Atonement

READ LEVITICUS 16

Write out step-by-step what happens on the Day of Atonement (also known as Yom Kippur).

READ LEVITICUS 23:26–32

What were the people of Israel supposed to do on this holy day?

DISCUSSION: Before going to the New Testament, what parallels do you see between this holy day and what Jesus did on the cross?

Jesus, Our Atoning Sacrifice

READ HEBREWS 9:1–28

What parallels does the author of Hebrews draw between Jesus and the "first tent"?

DISCUSSION: According to this passage, how is Jesus a "more perfect":

High Priest:

Sin Offering:

Scapegoat:

After reading this passage, why were God's plans for the Tabernacle so specific and the command to build exactly as instructed?

His Glory Dwells in Their Midst

READ EXODUS 40:34–38 AND LEVITICUS 9:15–23

Write a 2–3 sentence summary of these passages.

When did Israel know to stay?

When did Israel know to move?

DISCUSSION: After these seven weeks of study, we finally see God dwell in the midst of His people. What have you learned about the character of God through this? How do you want to respond?

His Glory Dwells in Our Midst

READ MATTHEW 27:50–51

What happens in this passage? (This is the Temple, but the pattern of the Holy Place and the Holy of Holies were similar, and the Veil held the same significance.)

DISCUSSION: When did this happen? What does this tell us about Jesus' death?

READ ACTS 2:1–41

Write a 2–3 sentence summary of this passage.

What similarities do you see in the coming of the Holy Spirit at Pentecost and God's glory filling the Tabernacle?

Where does God's glory now dwell?

Moving Forward

READ HEBREWS 10:19–27

What common language do you see in this passage and what we've studied in the Tabernacle?

What can we now do because of Jesus?

Reread vv. 26–27. Pray and ask the Holy Spirit to reveal how you should respond in your attitude, actions, or thoughts and live out the truths we've learned throughout the study.

Seeing God's character should cause us to see ourselves differently. What have you learned about yourself in this study?

To Dwell in our Midst

WEEK 7 NOTES

HOW SHOULD I RESPOND?

What is the final furnishing encountered in the Tabernacle? What was the purpose? What did this accomplish?

Write a prayer of praise and thanksgiving for how Jesus is the more and better atonement.

Because God is:

     I can:

TO Dwell IN OUR Midst

TEACHING NOTES

To Dwell in our Midst

TEACHING NOTES

To Dwell in our Midst

GROUP NOTES

TO
Dwell IN OUR
Midst

GROUP NOTES

To Dwell in our Midst

ADDITIONAL NOTES

THE BRONZE ALTAR

What it accomplished:

What it represents:

How it points to Jesus:

Cross-references:

THE BRONZE BASIN

What it accomplished:

What it represents:

How it points to Jesus:

Cross-references:

THE LAMPSTAND

What it accomplished:

What it represents:

How it points to Jesus:

Cross-references:

THE TABLE OF SHEWBREAD

What it accomplished:

What it represents:

How it points to Jesus:

Cross-references:

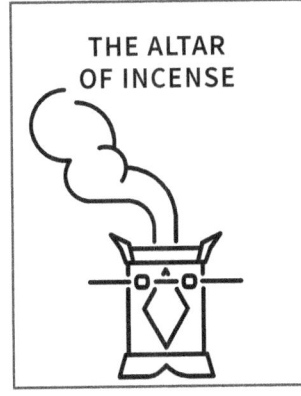

THE ALTAR OF INCENSE

What it accomplished:

What it represents:

How it points to Jesus:

Cross-references:

THE ARK OF THE COVENANT

What it accomplished:

What it represents:

How it points to Jesus:

Cross-references:

To Dwell in our Midst

ADDITIONAL NOTES

To Dwell in our Midst

ADDITIONAL NOTES

To Dwell in our Midst

ADDITIONAL NOTES

To Dwell IN OUR Midst

ADDITIONAL NOTES

To Dwell in our Midst

ADDITIONAL NOTES

To Dwell in our Midst

ADDITIONAL NOTES

141

The Sacrifices
(Answer key for page 46)

OLD TESTAMENT SCRIPTURE	TYPE OF OFFERING	PURPOSE	WHAT WAS OFFERED	NEW TESTAMENT SCRIPTURE	REFLECTING JESUS
Leviticus 1:1–4, 10, 14 **Leviticus 6:8–13**	Burnt Offering	To burn all night, completely consumed – showed total commitment to God – surrender & dedication	Bull, sheep, or goat, male without blemish, birds	**Romans 12:1–2**	Total surrender to God—complete devotion
Leviticus 2:1–3, 8–13 **Leviticus 6:14–18**	Grain Offering	Thanksgiving, praise, or memorial of what God had done, offering, part was burned, part was given to Aaron and sons as provision	Flour, oil, frankincense, unleavened	**Hebrews 4:15** **(see 1 Corinthians 5:6–8 for what leaven represents)**	Symbolized Jesus's sinlessness (leaven was symbolic of sin)
Leviticus 3:1–2, 6–8, 12–13 **Leviticus 7:11–13, 28–30**	Peace or Fellowship Offering	Recognized our ability to have fellowship and peace with God	Animal from the herd, lamb or goat, male or female, without blemish, included a communal meal	**John 6:53–58** **John 15:8–11**	We abide in Him, in Christ, we have life, one day we will have peace, we are reconciled to God, the Lord's Supper
Leviticus 4:1–3, 13–15, 22–24, 27–29 **5:1–7, 11** **6:24–25**	Sin Offering	To atone for sin (forgiveness of sin) and purify for uncleanness	**Priest:** Bull, **Whole Congregation:** bull, **Leader:** male goat, **Common People:** a female goat or female lamb, two turtle doves or pigeons	**Romans 5:1–11** **Romans 3:23**	The wages of sin is death—blood covers our sin; Christ sacrificed Himself to atone for our sins
Leviticus 5:14–16, 17–19 **6:1–7** **7:1–2**	Guilt Offering	Forgiveness of specific sins or against misuse of God's holy things	Ram without blemish	**Isaiah 53:4–6** **Colossians 1:13–14** **Ephesians 1:7–10**	Jesus is our guilt offering, took our iniquity, redeemed us, forgave our sins

feasting at the table

I love comfort food. I'm definitely not one of those girls who typically orders a salad. Give me meat and potatoes. One of my favorite comfort dishes is slow cooker pot roast. I love that I can throw a bunch of ingredients in a magical machine, and eight to ten hours later, I have an amazing meal. Even better, I love how my house smells when I've been gone all day, and I walk in at dinnertime to the most enticing scent.

Here's my beef (pun intended) with most pot roast recipes: they tell you to sear the outside of the roast first. Y'all. That defeats the purpose of a slow cooker meal! I know it adds flavor, but that's a time-consuming extra step I don't have time for in my busy morning. My recipe adds additional flavor in a couple of other ways. First, I don't add potatoes in the slow cooker and instead serve the pot roast alongside mashed potatoes. Potatoes cooked with the roast tend to taste like the roast, making it a one-note dish. Serving mashed potatoes on the side provides a creamy contrast in both texture and flavor. Second, I make a simple gravy to serve on top. It comes together super quickly as you are getting ready to eat, and it really is *so* simple and delicious!

While I do love meat, I do not love fatty meat. This is where you can tailor your choice to your family's preferences. I prefer an eye round roast, which is leaner than the typically used bottom round or chuck roast. I almost always wait until it's on sale at the grocery store. Also, feel free to add more vegetables (or less). You want to make sure you do not overfill your slow cooker so the lid sits properly on top, but if you have a larger slow cooker, by all means—fill it up!

Last little tip: you can chop up all the vegetables the night before so that in the morning, you can dump it all in and go about your day. Oh yeah, and don't forget to turn it on. It's no fun when you come home after a long day expecting your house to smell amazing and instead find a raw roast and now have to figure out a Plan B for dinner (not that I am speaking from experience or anything). Enjoy!

ERIN'S SLOW COOKER POT ROAST

Time: 8–10 hours (15 minutes of prep)
Yield: 6–8 Servings

INGREDIENTS
3–4 pounds eye round, bottom round, or chuck roast (fat trimmed)
10 whole carrots, peeled, ends trimmed, and cut into 2–3 inch pieces
6 stalks of celery, ends trimmed, and cut into 2–3 inch pieces
1 sweet onion, peeled, halved, then sliced
10 garlic cloves, peeled and smashed

3 bay leaves
1 teaspoon kosher salt
2 teaspoons thyme
a few cracks of fresh ground black pepper
½ cup low-sodium broth (vegetable, chicken, or beef)

INSTRUCTIONS
1. Place about half of the carrots, celery, onion, and garlic on the bottom of your slow cooker.
2. Place the roast on top of the vegetables. Sprinkle with salt, thyme, and pepper.
3. Add the remaining vegetables around the roast, making sure there are some onions and garlic on top of the meat.
4. Add the bay leaves.
5. Pour the broth over the meat.
6. Cook on low for 8–10 hours.
7. Serve with mashed potatoes and gravy.

Quick Gravy:
About 5 minutes before serving, melt 2 tablespoons of butter in a medium-sized skillet. Once melted, add 2 tablespoons of all-purpose flour and whisk for 1 minute. Add 2 ladles of liquid from the slow cooker. Whisk until there are no lumps. You can add more liquid to get the desired consistency. Salt and pepper to taste.

about Erin

ERIN H. WARREN is passionate about equipping and encouraging women to discover God's truths for themselves. She is the author of *Feasting on Truth: Savor the Life-giving Word of God*, leads and teaches Bible study through her ministry Feasting on Truth, and has published several Bible studies. She and her husband, Kris, have three littles (who aren't so little anymore), and they live in Central Florida. She loves a house full of people and a table full of food and hopes tacos never go out of style. You can find more information about Feasting on Truth on her website: FeastingOnTruth.com. You can also connect with her on Instagram: @erinhwarren and @feastingontruth and YouTube: www.youtube.com/c/erinhwarren.

146

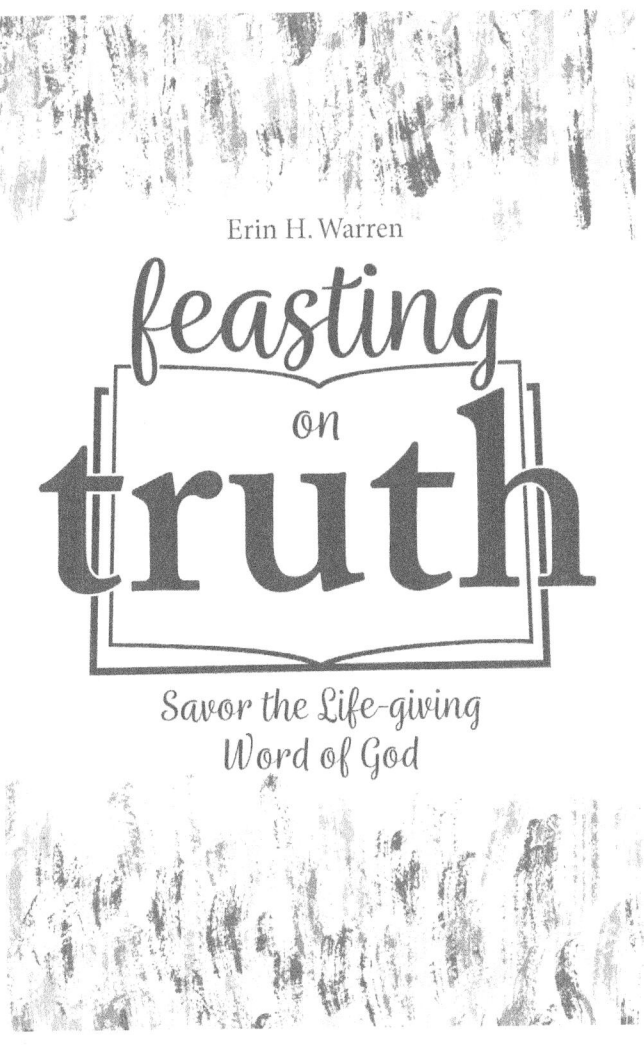

Erin H. Warren

feasting on truth

Savor the Life-giving
Word of God

FEASTING ON TRUTH

SAVOR THE LIFE-GIVING WORD OF GOD

The Word of God is our very life, but Erin Warren felt anything but alive. Her husband was sick. Her world was falling apart, and she had questions. Feel-good faith was not enough; she needed deep, sustaining truths.

Through her own wrestling, Erin Warren addresses the obstacles that held her back when it came to Bible study and how she discovered to savor the life-giving Word of God.

The word *feast* is rooted in abundance. That is what awaits us in the pages of Scripture: a table laid out before us, not only for our essential nourishment, but for our enjoyment.

FeastingOnTruth.com/Books

STORIES FROM THE WILDERNESS

A STUDY OF THE ISRAELITES' JOURNEY FROM EGYPT TO THE PROMISED LAND

The wilderness. It is a place that feels hard, empty, lifeless, and pathless, and it often leaves us with questions about who God is. But where we see a place that is worthless, confusing, and chaotic, God sees a place to display His power. Time and time again throughout Scripture, God takes the worthless, seemingly wasteful, confusing, chaotic, and empty places and uses them as a backdrop to prove His character, draw us in, and display His glory.

FeastingOnTruth.com/Wilderness

LIGHT & LIFE

AN INDUCTIVE STUDY ON PSALM 119

We hear it all the time: we need to read the Bible every day. But why is it so important that we know, understand, and apply this ancient book to our lives today? What's in it for us? In Psalm 119, we see over and over that God's Word brings life, and it's a light to guide us. If we truly knew the power the Word of God has in our lives, we wouldn't be able to put it down.

FeastingOnTruth.com/LightAndLife

WAYMAKER

AN ADVENT STUDY THROUGH THE BOOK OF HEBREWS

Jesus' coming was more than giving us forgiveness of sins or to part the way before us. He came to part the divide between God and us, between us and heaven. Jesus is the One who made a way to a restored relationship with God. No other book gives us a more comprehensive view of Jesus as our Way Maker than the book of Hebrews.

FeastingOnTruth.com/WayMaker

BY HIS GRACE FOR HIS GLORY

AN INDUCTIVE STUDY ON THE BOOK OF ROMANS

Romans is foundational yet deep. It's hard to understand yet simple. It is an incredibly powerful book that has been changing lives for centuries, and the truths in these sixteen chapters have the power to change our faith too. There are many familiar verses in Romans, and we associate this book with evangelism. But it is so much more! Discover what it looks like to live by His grace for His glory.

FeastingOnTruth.com/Romans